# Where Do Animals Live?

Alejandro Algarra / Rocio Bonilla

BARRON'S

# Where do animals live?

Kate and Jack are having fun playing with their pets. Their cat, Luna, looks like she wants to eat their fish! Cooper, the dog, hangs out in the play tent.

"Kate, I wonder if fish have homes in the sea, or if they just swim around," says Jack. "And, what about animals on land. . . where do they live?"

"I was just going to ask you if you knew where giraffes and zebras live!" replies Kate. "And, what about insects and spiders—do they have homes?"

"Good question," agrees Jack. "Let's check it out!"

# A place to live

Animals live in many different places. Their type of home depends on their daily lives and habits. Do they hunt or are they hunted? Do they have many babies or just a few? Do they care for their young or let them go off on their own? All of these things can affect where an animal lives or builds its home.

# How many places are there to live?

Think of all the places where animals can live. The list is huge! There are nests, caves, underground tunnels, webs, anthills, hives, tree trunks, lakes, rivers, and oceans. Some creatures even live under rocks! Can you think of any other places?

# Protected underground

Small mammals like rabbits, field mice, and shrews face many dangers living in the forest. To keep safe, they dig tunnels underground called dens or burrows. Once there, they are protected from skilled forest hunters, such as falcons, owls, foxes, and snakes!

# Living hidden

Inside their burrows, rabbits can care for their babies. Newborn rabbits have no fur, their eyes are closed, and their ears don't work very well, so the burrow protects them. But, a close cousin of the rabbit, the hare, has a very different way of life. Hares don't build burrows. Instead, they live hidden on the ground or under bushes. This is why hares are born with fur and open eyes—they are able to see when a hunter is coming and can flee to safety!

# Where would you put a giraffe?

Many large mammals never build a home. They live freely in the forest, on grasslands called the savannah, or in the jungle. Some live in groups and watch out for the arrival of hunters to warn the rest of the herd. Deer live in the American or European forests, while zebras, giraffes, and elephants all live freely in the African savannah and sleep wherever they are when they get tired. After all, it would have to be an incredibly big house to fit an animal as big as a giraffe or an elephant!

# Birds and nests

Flying birds, either alone or with their partner, look for tiny twigs, leaves, fur, and feathers to build their homes. They gather the items carefully and weave them together until they make a cozy nest. They build their nests in high places, such as trees and chimneys, where they can rest safely. The nest is also where they lay their eggs. When the chicks are born, they live protected inside the nest. The parents find food to feed the chicks until they are old enough to learn how to fly.

# Weavers, nest builders, and diggers

Not all birds build their nests in the same way. Weavers are a group of birds that make the most difficult nests in the world. Using the fibers from leaves and twigs, they weave nests shaped like baskets that they enter from below. Other birds build their nests with clay and saliva, such as swallows. There are even birds that dig nests in the soil or sand to protect their eggs underground. One of the biggest nests in the world is home to the American Bald Eagle. Its nest, which it builds in a tall tree, is large enough for a human to sit in!

# Living inside a tree trunk

A lot of animals make their homes inside of tree trunks. Woodpeckers not only peck into trees to hunt for yummy worms, but they also use their strong beaks to carve out holes where they can lay their eggs. Many other types of birds use the holes carved by woodpeckers to live in, or they look for natural holes in tree trunks. Squirrels, owls, and some bats also live in hollow tree trunks. Trees that have big openings at the bottom of their trunks are often home to large mammals like foxes or black bears.

# Wood for bugs

Insects also use wood as a place to live. The trunks, branches, and leaves of trees are ideal homes for insects and spiders. Small and large worms live inside tree trunks, and they build long tunnels where they can eat safely. Even bees build hives inside of tree trunks. If you think about it, a fallen tree trunk in the forest is the closest thing to a five-star hotel for little critters!

# A home made of silk

Spiders make silk to build their homes. They use the silk to weave webs so they can rest and catch food. The web is sticky and almost invisible, so flying insects become trapped. . . and then become dinner! Some spiders don't weave webs but instead use the silk to line tunnels in the ground. When their home is finished, they remain quietly inside with their legs touching the silken threads. If any walking bug is unlucky enough to step on the threads, the spider comes out of the tunnel and captures it. Too bad!

# Busy builders

If any animal deserves the title of builder, it's the ant! These tiny insects work together to build amazing homes underground known as colonies. We often see small mounds in the dirt called anthills. But, there is more than meets the eye. These anthills have many different living areas, just like a house! There are bedrooms, kitchens, nurseries, and more. Some ants build their colonies under large, flat stones. The stones soak up the heat from the sun during the day and keep the ants warm at night. Ants are so smart!

# Living in the sea

Many creatures that live in the sea have no home. Fish, whales, dolphins, squid, and jellyfish spend their lives swimming freely in the sea. But, there are sea creatures that build homes in the water. Stingrays live buried in the sand so they can hide while they hunt. Octopuses make their homes inside of holes they find in rocks. Other animals, like coral, build their own shell-like homes and join together to form colonies. The largest of these colonies are called reefs, and some are so big they can be seen from space!

# A home for two

Hermit crabs find their homes in a really cool way. When the time comes to go out and explore the world, a young hermit crab will look for the empty shell of a sea snail and crawl inside it. When the hermit crab grows and the shell no longer fits, it will leave it and search for a larger one. Sometimes a sea anemone, a sea creature that looks like a plant, will climb onto the shell of a hermit crab. The sea anemone attaches itself to the shell and gets a free ride! But, in return, the hermit crab is protected from hunters by the anemone's stinging tentacles—long limbs that contain poison!

# Cave-dwelling animals

Caves make great homes for lots of animals. They are cool in the summer, warm at night, and offer safety from bad weather and hunters. Large mammals, such as bears, use caves to hibernate in the winter. There are other creatures, like spiders and small insects, that never leave their caves. Nocturnal animals—animals that only come out at night— also live in caves. Bats are nocturnal animals that need a safe place to sleep during the day, so they hang upside down from the ceilings of caves, where most of their enemies can't reach them.

# Extreme homes

There are animals that live in places with really hot and really cold temperatures. Penguins in the South Pole spend most of their lives living in open spaces on the ice. But, they have thick feathers that help protect them from the cold. Sometimes they huddle together in large groups for extra warmth! In the desert, animals face the opposite problem.

To avoid the extreme heat of the desert, most animals that live there, such as fennec foxes and snakes, only come out at night. They spend the daytime hours in underground burrows to keep cool.

"Hey, Jack…it was fun learning about animal homes, but thinking about living in the desert is making me hot and thirsty!" says Kate.

"And I'm getting cold thinking about living on ice like a penguin!" replies Jack. "I want some hot cocoa."

"And I need water. Let's go!" suggests Kate.

# Parent guide

The types of homes animals live in depend on different factors: the type of animal, the characteristics of the climate, whether the animal is a predator or prey, and so on. There are some tiny animals that can live in very small spaces, like ants. Ants can develop a complete colony with just a few individuals inside a walnut shell. Large mammals that populate the African savannahs, such as giraffes and elephants, or those that inhabit the oceans, such as whales and dolphins, live with no home. Instead, they have habitats that span hundreds or thousands of miles. Some animals use materials from nature or materials that they make themselves to build their homes. Others simply take advantage of natural structures or move to "homes" that have been abandoned by their former residents. Following are some of the characteristics of animal homes.

## DENS OR BURROWS
Many animals live in dens or burrows underground. These can be simple single rooms with one entrance or complex burrows made up of numerous tunnels and rooms, with several entrances and exits. Rabbits inhabit these types of complex burrows. Inside their tunnels, rabbits and other small mammals are protected from inclement weather and predators, although they are always exposed to the danger of hunters that can enter them easily, such as snakes.

## BUILDING ANIMALS
There are animals that build their homes with materials that they make themselves. Spiders, for example, use their own silk to weave their webs or to line tunnels in the ground, holes in rocks, and tree trunks. They wrap their silk around the prey they capture, but they also use it to wrap and protect their eggs. Spiders aren't the only animals that use silk. Ants build an enclosed chamber made of leaves by using the silk that separates their larvae. This chamber serves as a refuge for the queen and the eggs and larvae. Other animals use mud to make their homes, such as insects like the potter wasp. Some other building materials that animals use include paper, which some wasps make by chewing on wood, or the wax that bees make from pollen to house their larvae.

## NESTS

A nest is the most common type of bird structure. To build a nest, birds gather different materials, either alone or with the help of their partner. The materials include little twigs, stems, leaves, bits of fur left by mammals in the forest, and the remains of human activity, such as string, thread, or plastic fiber. They carefully weave a cozy nest where they lay eggs and incubate them. The nest then serves as the home for their chicks until they are taught how to fly. Not all nests are the same, however. Some birds are not very meticulous, and they haphazardly assemble a nest using only a few twigs. Birds of prey tend to have these types of nests. There are other birds that weave nests like veritable works of art, using plant fibers as threads. Examples of this type of bird are the weaver birds of tropical Africa and Asia.

## HOMES IN TREES

Trees are outstanding places to build a home for many animals, both vertebrates and invertebrates. Tree canopies provide many points that can support birds' nests. They can also be the home to other tree-dwelling animals that consider the tree's branches and leaves to be their home. There are many examples, such as sloths, which rarely leave trees because they both live and feed in them. Many monkeys and lemurs also live among the tree branches. Some animals build their home in the wood of living tree trunks, such as woodpeckers and many insects, which drill into the wood to find food or lay their eggs. Some trees are hollow inside long before they die. These hollow spaces are excellent places for large animals, such as badgers or even black bears, as well as rodents, bats, owls, and social insects like bees, wasps, and ants. When the tree dies, the decomposing trunk will be used as food and shelter for thousands of tiny critters.

## HOMES IN THE WATER

Water is home to lots of different animals. Many fish, including sharks, spend their entire lives swimming in the sea without ever stopping to rest on the bottom. Water is also the domain of the large cetaceans, such as the blue whale, the finback, and the sperm whale, and of their ancestral enemy: the giant squid! Other fish use rocks or sand to hide themselves. Worms live in the sand and protect themselves inside tubes that they make themselves, as do mollusks, sea urchins, and starfish. Fish like the moray eel and the conger eel,

sea anemones, gorgonians, and bivalves like mussels and oysters also make their homes in rocks. Barnacles, which are also mollusks, and gooseneck barnacles, which are crustaceans, adhere to the rocks where the tide ebbs and flows on the coastline. One animal, the coral polyp, manufactures a skeleton that results in such a large structure when joined with thousands of other individuals over the course of many decades and centuries, that it can become an island or even a coral reef that is visible from space. In continental waters, such as freshwater lakes, ponds, rivers, and streams, we can find fish, insect larvae, mollusks, and even spiders that spin bell-shaped webs to create air bubbles where they can live.

## EXTREME HABITATS

Animals that live in extreme habitats have to find strategies to survive. In the Polar Regions, where snow and ice predominate, the low temperatures prevent the development of many species from milder climates. However, some of them manage to adapt and thrive despite the harsh conditions. Polar bears live on ice in regions near the Arctic Circle. They travel to hunt for prey, usually seals or walruses. Only the female digs out a den when it comes time to give birth to her cubs. They live in the den until the cubs are ready for the cold outside world. In the Antarctic, the emperor penguin lives on frozen islands and ice floes. Each penguin couple does not form a nest; rather its members take turns protecting the eggs between their feet, under the heavy blanket of warm feathers on their bellies. In deserts, such as the Sahara, the situation is the opposite: During the day, the temperatures soar so high that they are unbearable for almost any living being. Also, water is extremely scarce. The most cautious strategy for many species is to take shelter in dens, burrows, or tunnels during the hours when the sunlight and heat are the most intense. When the sun goes down, before the temperature drops too precipitously, the animals leave their homes to feed on plants or to hunt other animals. At dawn, they may take advantage of the little dew that forms to hydrate. This is the realm of desert snakes, the curious fennec fox with its long ears, and beetles.

First edition for the United States and Canada published in 2016 by Barron's Educational Series, Inc.

© Gemser Publications, S.L. 2015
El Castell, 38 08329 Teiá (Barcelona, Spain)
www.mercedesros.com

Text: Alejandro Algarra
Design and layout: Estudi Guasch, S.L.
Illustration: Rocio Bonilla

All inquiries should be addressed to:
Barron's Educational Series, Inc.
250 Wireless Boulevard
Hauppauge, NY 11788
www.barronseduc.com

ISBN: 978-1-4380-0894-3

Library of Congress Control No.: 2016930610

Date of Manufacture: April 2016
Manufactured by: L. Rex Printing Company Limited, Dongguan City, Guangdong, China

Printed in China
9 8 7 6 5 4 3 2 1